PETER FOERTHMANN

MYTH
CIRCUMNAVIGATION

A GOAL IN LIFE OR A DEAD END?

Copyright: © 2020 Peter Foerthmann
Editor: Erik Kinting – www.buchlektorat.net
Layout: Sabine Abels – www.e-book-erstellung.de
Illustrations & Cover: Inga Beitz–Svechtarov
Photos: S. 10, 18, 19, 20, 30, 29: Wolfgang Clemens
       S. 13: Volker Kissling
       S. 16, 17, 19, 21, 27, 37, 40, 41, 59, 93: Peter Foerthmann
       S. 26, 84: Tino Schumann
       S. 44, 53: Douwe Fokkema
       S. 56, 67: Wilfried Krusekopf
       S. 64: Inga Beitz–Svechtarov

Publisher: tredition GmbH, Halenreie 40-44, 22359 Hamburg,
       Germany

ISBN 978-3-347-17454-2 (Paperback)
ISBN 978-3-347-17455-9 (Hardcover)
ISBN 978-3-347-17456-6 (eBook)

CONTENTS

Die größten Feinde des Seglers…

GEWITTER

zuVIEL Wind

KEIN Wind

KONTAINER-SCHIFFE

120m

zu hohe Wellen

ROST & KORROSION

UV-Strahlen fressen ALLES!

Salz-wasser

Bewuchs

Leinen im Propeller

Seekrankheit

ungewünschte Mitbewohner

Wale?

böse Korallen-Riffe

Kondenswasser & Lecks

CIRCUMNAVIGATION # 1

HIGHS, LOWS AND MYTHS

Few utterances stir the soul and spirit of a sailor like the word "circumnavigation", the visible tip of a vast iceberg mighty enough in the mind of most seafaring folk to change careers, restructure financial priorities and fuel any number of dreams (or nightmares, as the case may be).

The possibility, the temptation, the challenge: call it what you will, there is something about the prospect of one day taking the long way home that can reach deep inside sailing people and profoundly affect their outlook on work, personal relationships and the wider world. Success and failure assume a completely different dimension: all else pales beside the challenge that awaits at sea.

Almost anyone contemplating a venture of this magnitude must expect to have to go at least a few rounds with their inner demons along the way. Sometimes a circumnavigation will be best tackled in partnership, but the adventure can quite easily become so all-consuming as to leave the participants with energy only for themselves. Indeed there can be few situations in the scope of human relations that expose the foundations of a relationship to such unforgiving scrutiny: at sea, isolated in a hostile environment, there are no hiding places and no emergency exits through which to beat an honourable retreat. Sometimes the pressures involved bring people closer together, but if the façade has already begun to creak, it is likely no end of lies or half-truths will keep it together on the rolling deep.

THE "WHY?" QUESTION

Sailors have a special affinity for freedom and nature, yearning for and embracing the untamed elements of the sea; for us the life afloat serves as foil and counterweight to the strains and complexity of 'ordinary' life ashore. This philosophy creates fertile ground for ambitious dreams, dreams with potential very quickly to take on an unanticipated life of their own. Left unchecked, such dreaming tends to lead inexorably to The Dream. And, for as long as The Dream remains no more than a pleasant retreat from the frustrations of everyday life, why not?

But what if The Dream demands to be taken seriously? How far can we allow it to develop? Where do we draw the line – for our own protection? The ability silently to adapt our dreams to our reality without feeling the need to justify our action to ourselves or others is a skill that comes with experience. Social pressures are no basis on which to embark on an adventure: that way lies almost certain failure.

Contemplating a circumnavigation is one thing; allowing the fact that one has even begun to entertain the notion of sailing around the world to become known outside one's own head is quite another. The thought, once uttered, has the power to cement or destroy long-term partnerships – and the repercussions tend to run and run either way. The idea ra-

pidly develops an energy of its own that can seldom be deflected. The scheduled day of departure then becomes a catalyst for the subsequent evolution of human relationships: all concerns that need to be aired need to be aired before this point – leaving it for the sea to bring them out promises nothing but pain.

The germ of the idea of sailing around the world can lie dormant for years in some people, while in others it quickly takes root and multiplies. In either case, the prospects for a happy prognosis depend to a very considerable extent on spotting where reality ends and dreaming begins – and it is here that I hope I might be of some assistance. Youthful enthusiasm is not always the best policy.

MYTHS
AND IDOLS

The idea of circumnavigating usually finds its way into the sailor's head through literary channels. The world has no shortage of dusty volumes documenting the triumphs and torments of those who, not content with living The Dream, came home to record the experience on paper (for posterity, for the benefit of those to come after them or perhaps just to help replenish the kitty). The works of men like Wilfried Erdmann, Rollo Gebhard and Bobby Schenk continue to hold sway over German bookshelves, not least because of the efforts of their publisher to keep them there untroubled by the output of newer exponents of the art (who might have more recent experiences to share). This money-for-old-rope arrangement, which offers clear advantages from a cost-benefit perspective, seems to suit both sides very well. Once again, I find myself reminded of Bobby Schenk's apt and amusing observation to me that it's easy to spot a successful publisher: he's the one slurping champagne out of the skulls of his authors.

The publishing trade has not entirely succeeded in locking up the market, however, and there remain plenty of other idols whose authenticity or humour, for example, have won for their nautical confessions

a place in the heart of the sailing readership (and implanted or nourished the thought of one day crossing the same waters). German-speaking readers need look no further than Tania Aebi, Wolfgang Hausner, Hugo Wehner or Burghard Pieske for unforgettable tales and a generous helping of dream scenarios ideally suited as an escape from the tribulations of everyday life. A feature common to all of the books is that they inspire dreams by granting the reader an insight into another world and fuelling the great "what if?" If they can do it, I could ... Couldn't I?

The book market's capacity for idols though follows strict economic rules defined by purchase price, the size of the potential readership (sailors and dreamers) and, not least, the number of significant annual events (birthdays, Christmas, etc.) for which easily obtainable gifts are required. The books, moreover, paint a predominantly positive picture that concentrates on the highlights and conveniently overlooks the dark side. Why would anyone take to print to focus on the negative aspects? Who has the courage to admit, perhaps, that the effort was not worthwhile – and who would publish them if they did?

In the German-speaking market at least, the manufactured scarcity of true sailor/author heroes means that new editions are often released with only minimal updating. On top of that, of course, we all have an inherent tendency to colour and reinterpret our experiences in a way that does not necessarily preserve the truth, the whole truth and nothing but. The possibility exists, in other words, that relying on books could leave the sailor with a mental image somewhat at odds with salty wet reality.

Ay, there's the rub: books may be good for inspiration, but when it comes to information, the diligent reader would also be well advised to consider other sources to help fill in the blanks (and while finding other sources of information might have been quite a challenge in the past, today the only problem is likely to be filtering the wealth of information available). Seasoning big plans with a generous serving of truth increases the chances of surviving the realities of bluewater life when they make their presence felt.

Or you can just hope for the best, but then everything comes down to pure luck.

Bluewater seminars too provide an excellent opportunity to close the gap between two worlds: the physical distance between chronicler and audience is minimal and, provided there is no stage, communication can proceed at a face-to-face level.

There seems no getting away from the fact that in Germany we have very few sailing heroes – a reflection, perhaps, of the status of our sport in a country so thoroughly obsessed with kicking strips of dead cow skin around a field. Bobby Schenk's "Who's who" of circumnavigators lists just 74 successful crews from the German-speaking world. While their number is really quite remarkably small, the valuable information to be gleaned from their answers to Bobby Schenk's standard set of ten questions should on no account be overlooked. The remarks introducing the list make interesting reading too, stressing as they do the elite nature of the achievement. It seems, without wishing in any way to diminish the personal exertions (and sufferings) of the perpetrators, that there is still an element of the magical to a successful circumnavigation. Are we dealing here with a club for the enlightened few or are these in truth ordinary people who find their undoubtedly out of the ordinary achievements recast retrospectively to fit some imagined hero status? Would-be circumnavigators would be well advised to ask the same questions of themselves.

The situation outside Germany is rather different. The book market in the USA, for example, is enormously fertile by comparison, mainly because a much larger proportion of authors there publish and market their books and eulogies themselves. Which is tough for the publishers, good for the authors and a boon for readers, who have the opportunity to find out all about what they might be getting into while there is still time to mould and adapt their own plans.

SCALING THE HEIGHTS, SURVIVING THE MUNDANE

Some circumnavigators clearly regard a full circle of the earth as the crowning glory of their life. People have an instinctive urge to stand out from the crowd and some circumnavigators undoubtedly come to view their achievement as the keystone of what makes them exceptional, what elevates them above the huddled masses. When someone of this persuasion puts pen to paper, the chances of the ego wresting control of the editorial process (leaving reality floundering in its wake) are self-evidently very high.

People aiming to make money by or from sailing, moreover, face a strong temptation to stretch the truth a little, to set themselves apart from the fleet and gain the sort of marketing leverage that might persuade a publisher to add their name to that list of favoured authors. Shifting nautical books at the prices usually applied is no easy business without an artificially limited range and, perhaps, some embellishment of the tale here and there.

The experience of circling the globe by boat has a profound effect on that vast majority of circumnavigators who feel no irresistible urge to condense their adventure into book form for posterity. Daunting it may be in terms of absolute scale, but at a fundamental level The Dream itself is straightforward and simple to grasp. The reality (as sober reflection

might suggest) is much more complex and those who have experienced it first-hand not surprisingly tend to see things from a rather different perspective. It is said – whisper it gently – that some sailors, humbled by the challenges survived, have actually been over-joyed to see home again.

Once at sea, the well-read sailor cannot help but end up comparing his or her own daily life with the content of the various literary efforts browsed and processed back on dry land. The yawning gulf between the two generally makes itself apparent very quickly: often it doesn't take much practical experience at all to leave the myths of finely worded theory holed below the waterline. The same process soon reveals the heroes of yesterday to be ordinary mortals after all too. As WOLFGANG CLEMENS, an irreverent and hugely experienced feature of the German bluewater scene since 1987, once succinctly put it:

I've caught them all telling stories

SAILOR´S BLOGS

My recommendation for sailors interested in prolonged voyaging is to leave the classics of sailing literature on the shelf and spend more time reading blogs, which have the additional benefit of coming in much more easily digestible servings. Bloggers seem much less susceptible than book authors to the temptation of trying to be an expert in everything too, perhaps because they just don't have the same need to big themselves up. I am struck time and again by the way certain authors repackage the expert knowledge of specialists in their writing as if it were their own: including a source reference for information in no way diminishes the person citing the source, quite the opposite. Accepting that there are limits to our knowledge is not a character flaw (unless the person doing the accepting is professing ignorance of how all that tax liability disappeared).

Sailor's blogs, of which there are thousands to be found, provide a wonderful insight into the inner state of our peers in the process of reconciling their dreams and reality. Untainted by any profit motive, they generally ooze honesty and authenticity too. Good examples of the genre include the blogs of SV TAMORA and SV AKKA

My bluewater portal provides access to thousands of yacht blogs ordered by

    – SHIPS´S NAME from A – Z
    – Catamaran Blogs
    – Sailing author blogs
    – Circumnavigator blogs

A NUMBER UNKNOWN

The number of sailors who failed to complete their planned circumnavigation for whatever reason over the last decade must run into the thousands even just here  in Germany. I will come back to the question of why this should be later on. Suffice it to say at this point that everyone has the right to freedom of thought and that all humane reasons are understandable and worthy of respect. I would not deny, however, that there are some who seek and find in the failures of others a reason – or excuse – to stay at home themselves too.

Indeed I am sure it is entirely possible for sailors to follow the mishaps of others online from the comfort of their own sofa and effectively talk themselves out of even risking the same mistakes themselves (actually perhaps this is just the elegant emergency exit required as the day of departure draws near and fear threatens to take control). Those with less backbone can always find solace in a convenient excuse, swiftly transforming their own problem into someone else's.

THE LIFE PLAN

Much has been written about the ideal time in life to sail around the world. I have no interest in commenting on how people choose to organise the various elements of their life and even if I did, life tends to write its own rules anyway with no respect for our plans however carefully laid. All I will say is that a sabbatical year – a privilege most commonly accessible in Germany to those nourished at the public trough – will suffice only for sailors circumnavigating non-stop in a professional capacity (lured perhaps by the prospect of fame and fortune and pursued day and night by relentless sponsors eager to extract the maximum return). Across the Atlantic and back makes a more reasonable trip for a sabbatical year (although the Baltic is also always an option for those wishing to stay closer to home). Sailors who find themselves employed in the private sector are unlikely to be able to follow the sabbatical route unless they happen to have particularly rare and valuable skills, in which case they might get lucky.

Even now many sailors set out on the (initially) well-trodden path that leads to the seven seas only by way of education, career, family and, finally, the long wait until the next generation at last finds a way to stand on its own two feet. The idea is that with life's 'work' accomplished, he and she redeem their ancient promise and set sail, but as I'm sure most of us recognise only too well, the intervening decades throw up so many choices and so many imponderables that few entrants make it even as far as the starting line.

Over the years I have heard countless tragic tales of how cruel twists of fate – everything from illness and divorce to insolvency and insurmountable problems with the children – have left sad ships abandoned in far-flung locations, the proceeds of their emergency sale at a knock-down price the only consolation for the deflated souls left struggling with the painful realisation that they spent too long chasing a false dream.

GOING IT ALONE

Crew size numbers tend to be decided by life rather than on sailing grounds (unless, of course, the trip is planned principally as a solo spectacular for external consumption and the presence of a partner would dilute the drama). While I would not in any way wish to diminish the voyages completed by singlehanders, I remain convinced that people deal most effectively with the challenges of an unforgiving sea as part of a team. I need hardly add, of course, that not everyone is fortunate enough in life's lottery to find a partner with whom the round-the-world adventure can be shared and genuinely enjoyed. For more about the singlehanded option see here.

The list of possible sailing records for singlehanders has shrunk considerably of late, not least because everyone understands that records now often have little to do with raw curiosity and exploring the limits of personal capabilities and a great deal more to do with feeding the voracious media, which need first-hand accounts to keep the wheels of commerce turning and for which talk of dreams, challenges, the burning desire to triumph against the odds is no more than a convenient cover story to conceal the synthetic and fundamentally pointless nature of the undertaking.

When sailors backed by commercial sponsors and investors embark on extreme voyages with the aim of gaining exposure for marketing purposes, seamanship is often the first casualty: who needs to be careful when the first sniff of an emergency brings the helicopter racing over, bristling with photographers poised to capture the moment for maximum media leverage?

On the other hand, many male singlehanders undoubtedly still find themselves drawn to bluewater sailing by more primordial motivations, typically some variation on the age-old dream of the South Sea reclining among the swaying palms; for them the time at sea often amounts almost to an interlude, a time to draw breath between long periods ashore during which they are usually anything but alone. Swiss retired airline pilot Otti Schmid remains a favourite example of this more relaxed, hedonistic approach and his amusing reports from the front line are always worth a read.

Without wishing to rain on anyone's parade, I should add a word of caution at this point for any solo sailors contemplating a prolonged stay on land in New Zealand, Australia or Brazil: lone wolves tempted by the exotic pleasures of a native honeypot should bear in mind that shacking up with anyone – formally or otherwise – for more than 24 months in any of these countries can be a very quick way to shed half your assets. This public service message has been brought to you by liveaboard Ingo B., who tells me he very nearly careered off this particular cliff himself.

MONEY

Let me begin by confirming that there is little possibility these days of funding a trip around the world out of money earned informally along the way. Writing books seldom does much for the bank balance and the same applies to blogs. While it is possible in theory to make money from blogging, by selling advertising space and promoting sponsors, modern internet users know click bait when they see it and understand that objectivity and profitability make uncomfortable bedfellows in the blogosphere. We need look no further than the BERNT LUECHTEN-BORG case for a sobering example of what can go wrong – for sailor and backers alike – when experiences at sea become too tightly intertwined with the pursuit of our daily bread.

Alex & Taru may well be the exception that proves the rule. Their blogs have earned them quite a measure of fame, although Taru's passion for fashion and her enthusiasm for  sharing photos of herself unencumbered by more than a minimum of clothing give them an edge few can match.

Not everyone has this kind of capital on board – and the fact that their "new" boat, a stunning Herreshoff classic, is at least as eye-catching as her lady owner certainly does no harm either.

Pay-to-sail, be the paying guests family, friends, acquaintances or total strangers, can be a risky way to finance a trip and requires both very careful planning and a bigger boat than would otherwise be necessary. Anyone contemplating this route would do well to read up on the relevant legal niceties in likely countries of landfall too. While being boarded on arrival by booted elephants in uniform sounds bad enough, there exists a very real possibility in parts of the world of being unable to "invite" a guest to disembark at the end of an excruciating passage without also having to provide them with a free ticket for the flight home. Visitors aboard have a tendency (at least when they are paying) to plan their flights well in advance for cost reasons, moreover, which can play havoc with routing and create an intractable conflict of interests in the event of unfavourable weather. Trying to keep up with someone else's itinerary is never a recipe for success.

No matter how close the relationship between owners and guests, the presence of visitors on board – even the dearly-beloved family – can very easily become very tedious indeed. The best visits of course – and this applies irrespective of whether the visitor is paying guest or friend – are those that end before we want them to. The sense that the main attraction of your floating pride and joy is its ability to provide free holiday accommodation can easily see visitors who arrived in the guise of friends leave as no more than acquaintances.

Jobs ashore remain the better alternative. Hourly rates will never amount to much, but bodies – and languages – are always in demand all over the world in the tourist industry. Sailors with the relevant skills always have the option of working for their less skilled but better funded fellow travellers too, but this can amount to little more than slavery if the local yards and service companies have already stitched up the market. This kind of work also carries with it the risk of upsetting the natives and it seems to be by no means unusual for local monopolists to stifle competition from visiting sailors with a quiet word to the police, security services or border control. Recently one yacht in the Canaries was found to have a cockpit full of sawdust and wood shavings. The occupant, it transpired, was recharging the coffers by working as a carpenter.

Ultimately the fact remains that most circumnavigations are funded out of savings, the proceeds of letting property or other forms of income. Finance never ceases to be a challenge: the collapse in interest rates in recent years, for example, has forced a great many sailors to change or postpone their plans.

THE PERFECT BOAT

The perfect boat for sailing around the world really needs to have a metal hull. The only choice to be made is whether to go with aluminium or steel and this tends to be decided by the capital available.

A metal hull can survive grounding, stranding and the crushing embrace of the ice. A GRP hull, no matter how enthusiastically reinforced, stands about as much chance as a fish in the desert when push comes to shove (just take a moment to see what the experts prefer in France and the Netherlands, for example). Plastic boats can and do make it safely all the way around, of course, but only if lady luck smiles on them. It really is that simple.

ALL THE WAY?

And so we approach the heart of the matter: round the Atlantic or round the world? Political considerations – social conventions among sailors – the hazards to be faced on the world's oceans – safety in numbers – transporting the boat home – selling the boat abroad: all this and more we will consider in Part 2,

promises
Peter Foerthmann

CIRCUMNAVIGATION # 2

ALL THE WAY AROUND
... WHAT?

Haparanda: remote, mysterious, alluring... and located at the very top of the Baltic, so best enjoyed with the aid of some friendly sunshine. It's really all about the journey, as every wise mariner knows, but even so some people need guaranteed sun and warmth to get them out of their bunk and for them a tour of the Med might be more appropriate (although a better relationship with the sun does come at the price of a trickier relationship with the wind, which tends in these lower latitudes to come in just the two sizes: too little and too much). But then every silver lining has its cloud, of course, and with that in mind I would now like to cast a critical eye over the routing options....

While not without its challenges, the well-trodden path to the Caribbean is hard to overlook. Wind on the quarter, sun from all sides: that's sailing how they sell it in the brochure. Off the beaten track it isn't, but even today the Caribbean undoubtedly has what it takes to set our dreams soaring. It has its disadvantages too (as a certain type of congenital-ly grumpy sun-deprived Northern European seems to take pleasure in explaining), but there is a strong case to be made for learning about them first-hand!

A few alternatives (all standard disclaimers apply):
- Stay a second season (this may include one or more games of hide-and-seek with angry forces of nature, so check the insurance)
- A trip up and down the East coast of the US (plenty to see, a fair chance of rain and easy access at all times to major airports with good links home for births, deaths and marriages)
- The short way back to the old world (this programme can cast a long shadow over a crew's sojourn in paradise because the clock never stops ticking – the whole experience risks becoming a race from island to island, waypoint to waypoint with never enough time to stop and feel the sand between your toes)
- A deep breath and on through the Panama Canal into a whole new dimension of opportunities, possibilities and dilemmas. Enter the Pacific and Polynesia, still the non plus ultra of destinations, becomes a real possibility – the mystique, the remoteness, the intensity of sky and sea and, for the unreformed single gentleman, the hula girls (will dance for money)

New Zealand and Oz are hard to miss too (the ancients found them without so much as a pocket map) and the voyage to their shores – days and weeks at the mercy of the West Pacific and its capricious weather patterns – provides ample opportunity for every last soul on board to learn the value of humility. Resistance is useless!

Wonderful countries, vast distances... the thought of exploring the land away from the coast as well can become very enticing if the seed of the idea is once allowed to take root. Unfortunately though there are also inconveniences to consider, not least visas (never long enough), customs duties (always too high) and other encounters with the spectre of petty officialdom (polite enough on the outside, in the main, but sufficiently well-versed in the subliminal arts to leave visiting sailors in no doubt as to who holds all the cards). All of which explains why so many yachts shy away from running the gauntlet and turn again (and again and again) for another lap of the South Seas. The years pass and the same old questions continue to go unanswered until eventually the elephant in the room becomes too large to ignore: "How on earth do we get home safely from here?!?"

Down there, far from home on the other side of the world, sailors from all over the Northern Hemisphere find themselves confronted sooner or later with the need to make a decision: where – and what – next? Extended overland adventures offer sailors a completely different perspective and some conclude at this point that they have the best of their bluewater days behind them. The realities of a life afloat catch up with everyone in the end, don't they? Some thrive on them, some consider them a price worth paying and some find in the end that their time at sea has only heightened their fondness for the things they miss (not least the chance to relax and enjoy all that the world of dry land has to offer without the need always to put the ship first).

Some people crave variety, an outlet. In 'normal' life, sailing represents that outlet, but what happens when sailing itself becomes normal life? What of the far-travelled sailor whose nostrils have begun to crave the scents of land? The change – in outlook, attitudes, priorities, desires, objectives – can creep over people quite imperceptibly over the course of prolonged periods at sea, but it is nonetheless ir-resistible. That particular genie is not for re-bott-ling. There are chroniclers out there no doubt who will take great umbrage at this and insist I have got it wrong and that the myth (the myth they chased themselves perhaps) and the reality are one and the same. Indisputably there are people who set sail fully intending to go all the way around and then simply have a change of heart along the way, especially when it begins to feel as though the best is behind them.

Why deny it? What Pyrrhic victory awaits those who press on for the sake of an idea long after their love for the life has gone?

WHAT NEXT?

If, on the other hand, the love remains strong, the question of how to navigate a safe passage home through the geopolitical complexities of the modern world cannot be ignored for ever. There are dangerous waters ahead, as seafarers of various persuasions have had forcefully brought home to them in recent years. German circumnavigators Eva Hauer and Rüdiger Tamm SV Sola Gracia for example, were still struggling to come to terms with their experiences in the Indian Ocean and Red Sea on Sola Gracia (two yachts close by attacked by pirates, four Americans murdered, another group including children held hostage) some time after arriving home and resuming life on dry land. Stories of piracy, many of them with awful consequences for the mariners involved, have become all too common over recent years (for those with an appetite for tragedy, see WORLD OCEAN REVIEW

PIRACY:
THE WRITING ON THE WALL

The threat of piracy looms large for today's circum-navigators and largely explains why so many sailors seem to run into a dead end in the Far East, Australia, New Zealand, the Philippines, Malaysia and Thailand. The number of boats parked up in far-flung sailors' meeting grounds while their crews – anxious to be moving on but even more anxious about what that might entail – wait for something to break the deadlock has been growing steadily for years. And as everyone must surely have noticed, the passage of time has not made the appearance of a safe path home any more likely.

The well-known trouble spots barring all of the obvious routes can make the prospect of onward progress in a typical sailing boat – a lightly-canvassed snail, in effect – seem as attractive as Russian roulette in the rain. In an age when even the smallest fishing boat or fast rib can easily be tricked out with the latest communication systems and gadgets, sailors make an easy target for unscrupulous types prepared to offer violence for profit. The kidnap of Stefan O. and Henrike D. in the Philippines in April 2014, for example, remains unresolved and we can only hope that diplomacy will bring a happy ending sooner rather than later.

Political developments in the powder keg that is the Middle East have obviously made a nonsense of any passage plans featuring the Red Sea and Suez Canal, but in Malaysia too, piracy has become a major concern and fast-moving small boats now need to be monitored very carefully to avoid the possibility of unwanted and unpleasant consequences. Beate and Detlev Schmandt SV Kira von Celle recently made the hazardous passage to Langkawi themselves with Kira von Celle. They are still recuperating after the stress of this particular leg of their trip and have yet to decide whether – and if so how – to continue.

I once knew a man on a world tour with a production GRP 36 footer who consider himself invincible because he'd fitted bulletproof glass hatches...

The number of boats on standby at the other end of the world confirms in unmistakeable fashion that the global sailing community has taken the hard facts on board.

OPTIONS AND SOLUTIONS

COURSES

The way out for crews with the courage and capacity for a long, hard slog leads out far from land to South Africa and from there up to Brazil/the Caribbean and, eventually, the familiar waters of home. The shorter – and even tougher – option via Cape Horn remains largely the preserve of racers driven on by the unrelenting sponsors' whip (and even they now usually have virtual waypoint "ice gates" to keep them away from the growlers). Both options promise a world of worry and discomfort for average circumnavigators, who tend not to view their voyage first and foremost as a sporting challenge and will not necessarily have procured or prepared their boat with such an extreme adventure in mind. Excursions this far off piste (and I say this without malice or prejudice – every crew has to make its own decision based on its own preferences and capabilities) really do separate the wheat from the chaff in terms of both boats and crew. The days of a relatively easy passage back to the Med through the Suez short cut certainly seem to be off limits for the foreseeable future.

RALLYING ROUND

Jimmy Cornell very much had his finger on the pulse when he launched the ARC in 1986. Originally a family event fuelled by enthusiasm and improvisation and delivered with the aid of like-minded volunteers, Jimmy's idea has since spawned a worldwide rally industry involving all kinds of different event organisers that between them offer everything short of cruises around the local swimming pool and buyer guidance for prospective Oppi sailors. The now familiar bluewater seminars first became established as a key element in the train of this new "guided sailing" movement.

A list of the various rallies around the world can be found here.

Jimmy Cornell has recently returned to global rally organising after a long hiatus.

The geopolitical developments that not so long ago laid waste to the plans of whole armadas of sailors simultaneously created fertile ground for the rally business, which holds out the promise of safety in numbers as well as the social contact so many in the sailing community fear they might otherwise miss on longer trips. Only those who have experienced the rally model first-hand will understand fully what it entails and, most importantly, whether or not it works for them. None of the alternatives is without

its drawbacks, of course, and such rallies are clearly growing ever more popular in bluewater circles; so much so in fact that entry numbers are often limited – and often limited to the harbour capacity of the destinations to be visited.

The scene in Las Palmas every November provides a snapshot of the rally experience, enabling anyone interested in the prospect to grasp the impact of 250 boats and their more than 1200 crew on harbour facilities, parties and clubs. Suffice to say it takes some getting used to (and not everyone will want to get used to it). The party atmosphere starts to give way to a more serious build-up after a while, however, and once at sea there is peace at last.

A glance at the long list of sponsors (See here or here or here, for example) shows what a big business the rally industry has become: these days event partners and supporters come aboard not out of neighbourly goodwill but because they can smell the profits to be made. Even hotels and airlines have signed up as sponsors (participants, friends and family need flights and beds, do they not?). Add in the contributions of tourist boards, harbour and marina operators, local service providers and technical support providers for participants and the organisers and we must be looking at a market worth millions. Now let me think ... Who is ultimately going to foot that bill (see here, here or here)?

The marketing looks after itself too: the nautical press ensures plenty of coverage, with journalists flown out and hosted by the event organisers (just to make sure they arrive safely of course). The journalists get their story (and their free holiday), the magazines their content and the event organisers their exposure. It's a classic win-win, if you like (not me), the effect of which is to prise more sailors up out of the sofa to swell the ranks of the rally fleet – which is, after all, the object of the exercise. Interestingly though, as the size of the rally fleet has grown, so too has the number of boats choosing to shadow its progress – and share in its perceived safety in numbers – without becoming paid up customers.

Starting in 2015, World Cruising will be offering a round-the-world rally run on an annual cycle, enabling sailors to take a break when the need arises and return in time to continue with the next wave. For an eye-catching fee, a small, elite group of (generally quite large) boats is served up a full social programme, including press and parties, fit to fill every moment between arrival in one dream destination and departure for the next. The impact of these events on the venues they visit creates a certain amount of friction within the international sailing community, as the arrival of the elite fleet into port can leave everyone else feeling like second class citizens. Take Las Palmas once again, for example: the fleet descends and the 'ordinary' sailors find themselves shooed away by the harbour master into jam-packed anchorages to wait until the rally sets off and the pontoons free up again.

Unlike the ARC, which is timed to fit in with Christmas and the start of the charter season in the Caribbean and consequently attracts great squadrons of charter yachts, the US West Coast's Baja Ha-Ha has managed to retain its family feel.

The nature of their craft and their choice of parking spots may have betrayed the underlying differences in budget to the educated eye, but for decades bluewater sailors of all stripes formed part of the same harmonious (if rather loose-knit) community. No longer! The modern hot spots for charter fleets and key transit points for rally sailors have witnessed far-reaching changes as residents and prices adapt to a different type of sailor-customer with different demands, different priorities and – a regular source of tension – different ways of behaving.

Charter boats loaded with clowns in holiday mode have a completely different agenda to the ordinary cruising crew with the time and interest to explore properly what each port of call and its people have to offer.

The wider sailing community has now begun increasingly to avoid certain destinations as a result of increases in prices and 'upgrades' to facilities demanded by event organisers (backed up by the threat, implicit or otherwise, of taking their hordes elsewhere if their needs are not met). Anyone dubious as to the power wielded by event organisers need look no further than the evolution of the marina in Las Palmas: for decades a scene of desolation and decay, today it wants for nothing (excepting users – it only ever seems to be fully utilised for a few weeks of the year, presumably because ordinary sailors do not feel its much-enhanced facilities justify its also much-enhanced charges). The decrepit old one-way-ticket crawlers that used to pass through from time to time have become a rare sight indeed in today's Las Palmas!

Returning (for a moment at least) to the main thread of our investigation here, the question for us is whether sailing as part of a rally takes the risk out of dangerous passages. Given the current security situation in the world's various political flashpoints, I think the answer must be clear to all. It is difficult to imagine any rally organiser being able to cope with the scale of liability involved. I recently asked Jimmy Cornell about this directly, but he was reluctant to go into much detail despite the fact that the website for his BLUE PLANET ODYSSEY still shows a route through the Red Sea. Perhaps he will be able to find a way to beat the odds?

SPECIAL DELIVERY

Hiring a delivery crew to bring the boat home requires exceptional trust and a faith in mankind of a magnitude seldom seen today: your boat disappears from view for months on end and with opinions as to what constitutes due care varying so widely from person to person, you have no idea what surprises may be waiting when it rematerialises.

SALE not SAIL

It gives me no pleasure to say it, but the option of trying to sell a boat lying on the other side of the world also entails a world of trouble. You might manage to find potential buyers who are interested enough to fly out (all expenses paid?) and inspect the merchandise and they might like what they see, but even then there is still the potential problem of the local customs authorities to overcome. In fact even simply leaving a boat in another country for a prolonged period can turn into a game of cat and mouse with the authorities, which know only too well there could be money to be made. Tax collectors the world over seem to have a particular interest in sailing boats and it can take considerable guile – or the services of a tax expert or lawyer – to elude their clutches. One person who cannot expect to make much money out

of a boat sold far from home is the seller (an over-view of the Reinke yachts for sale around the world can be found here). Market forces are merciless and very few boats sold in far-flung locations bring in anything close to the owner's original asking price.

One person's misfortune is another's opportunity, however: in France, there are liveaboard families that roam the world looking for bargains they can sail back to Europe or the US and sell on – always through a broker – for a profit. I imagine it must be an addictive lifestyle for someone with the nerve, a little capital and a sufficiently free-spirited mindset to embrace this itinerant existence, family and all. For someone with the right background, the necessary knowledge of boats and access to willing hands, this unusual way of life could represent an attractive way to spend a few years on the move cheaply without growing stale or losing the love for sailing.

CARGO

Shipping your boat home as cargo is not as daft an idea as it might at first seem. The cost is not insignificant, but the benefits – provided one is honest about the alternatives – may well make it worthwhile all the same. A standard 40 ft container from Japan to Hamburg still costs less than US$ 1,000, although a fine sailing yacht will of course cost rather more (especially if the hard-nosed contractors of the commercial shipping world get wind of the fact they are dealing with an amateur – that's manna from heaven in their eyes). I once had a 28ft powerboat delivered from Ft. Lauderdale to Mallorca on a float-on/float-off for US$ 5,000, which is precisely US$ 7,500 less than the price initially quoted to me in writing six days earlier. Prices go into free fall as the time of departure draws near, in other words, because at that point every additional order is seen as a welcome bonus. Clearly though this is no strategy for the faint-hearted!

Once the decision has been made that just sailing on home is not going to work, the yacht transport option is well worth investigating (see here or here and perhaps also here or even here). Not only do you have your boat back on home waters quickly for your own use, but you will probably also find yourself in a much healthier market should your next move be to sell the boat. And thankfully today it is entirely possible to put your boat on another boat for transport by sea and still hold your head high around the marina and yacht club; indeed I know of a number of brave souls who chose this very solution even though it was never mentioned in the books.

THE DEAD END

Is my message then that trying to sail all the way around the world is no longer wise – or even no longer possible? The facts are there for all to see and I leave each to draw his or her own conclusions. The decision to pass through the Panama Canal is a biggie because from here on in, things get serious: the price of flights home becomes excruciating, visitors have to endure endless hours in the sky and airport lounges and while paradise awaits, it offers only a temporary distraction from the perils to come. People need to have a Plan B in mind in good time if those heady days among the palms are not to deteriorate into uncertainty and anguish.

What began with the occasional seafaring adventurer has now become the subject of mass tourism. Even serious authors will have us believe high-volume production yachts are up to the challenge of a circumnavigation. Modern navigation and communication technology has greatly reduced the fear factor that accompanies the dream of setting out on the great round the world adventure, furthermore. Once upon a time every sailor had to be his or her own mechanic, but thanks to SailMail people with problems afloat now have access to dozens of virtual helplines and service engineers all over the world.

The nature of the typical bluewater sailor has changed over time too (if I can make such an observation without sounding too curmudgeonly), not least because the matter of available resources now plays such a big role. Money is no substitute for knowledge and experience at sea, of course, indeed some would say one of the great beauties of the sea is its capacity as a leveller, that way it reminds us that all of us are no more than so much spindrift. A quick look at how boats and equipment have changed over the decades though suggests the very notion of adventure has changed beyond all recognition. We sail in an age when the failure of a tool previous generations could scarcely have imagined – networked autopilots, GPS or AIS, for example – can trigger disaster. Truly the service society has taken to the waters and is crowing in plain sight at just what people can achieve in the modern world without actually lifting a finger themselves.

Many sailors (principally the experienced ones) still have the insight to understand the other side of the coin, however, to appreciate that every factor on which they rely at sea – right down to their own courage and capabilities and, above all, the toughness of their craft – has its limits. An honest appraisal of where these limits lie will naturally cause some to hesitate, to revisit and perhaps revise their plans. I consider this a process of natural selection and a thoroughly good sign: it shows that the lessons of a lifetime's experience are still at the helm of the decision-making exercise. The inexperience (or is it pride?) of sailors who knowingly avoid acknowledging – and exploring the consequences – of their own limits promises nothing but trouble at sea, especially if this

foolhardiness is exacerbated by hopes of making money from the venture.

Some will tell a different tale for sure but to my mind, now is just not an opportune time to be sailing around the world. Experience teaches us to think carefully and rationally about important decisions and one of the great strengths of the rational mind is its ability to drop or reorganise even long-standing plans if the risks become too pronounced. But what if the genie is already too far out of the bottle? What of the yachtsman whose friends, neighbours, colleagues and postman have all heard the grand plans and who cannot now see any way to back out and still save face? For people who find themselves in this position there remains one final, compelling argument to consider: ultimately you face the sea alone, with nobody to hold your hand and nobody to make things happen but you.

The constant worry about the delicate little anchor and the big fat boat dangling from it, the subtle piracy of the local port authorities, the endless visa dance, the terror of the weather forecast, the challenge of provisioning without importing stowaways of the four-, six- or eight-legged variety, antisocial social contacts, the never-ending list of boat jobs, the relentless burning sun... A trip around the world makes a wonderful dream if only reality doesn't intrude too far.

The rapid expansion of the charter business around the world is no accident: many sailors like being able to realise their dreams one step at a time without having to worry about the bigger picture. An enormous number of sailors spend years afloat without ever venturing much beyond Southern Europe, moreover, suggesting that perhaps here too, wiser heads have eventually prevailed. And then of course we have the countless sailors who have grown tired of the Southern sun and retreated to home waters in the higher latitudes.

I have no desire to put a damper on anyone's wanderlust. But there are spectacular destinations aplenty to explore in the more secure parts of the world if only we can shake off this myth that seems to hold us so tightly in its grasp: the myth of a carefree circuit of the Earth punctuated with beautiful bays for all to share and simple-minded locals with no other concerns than trading coconuts for glass beads.

Circumnavigation is no longer the top tip for sailors who put enjoyment first. There are just too many parts of the world now where – properly serious – serious stuff threatens to get in the way of the fun, suggests (with a measure of irony and an eye to his own shortcomings),

Peter Foerthmann

CIRCUMNAVIGATION # 3

IN OUR DREAMS

Waterproofs, I would suggest, do not to feature much in most dreams of sailing around the world: fair winds, following seas and capable, entertaining (as you will) and steadfast company are much more the order of the day. Reality likes to paint a rather different picture, however, taking events – and with them relationships – in directions we never intended. Sometimes this just counts as part of the fun, but sometimes people find themselves having to re-

ach an accommodation with their life rather than actively living it, at which point the bluewater dream becomes a solo exploit (or the boat stays at home).

We live in a world that likes to commoditise dreams, to package them up as fodder for marketing gurus, publishers and the media, which then sell them on in carefully sanitised form in an exercise that brings the cash rolling in while simultaneously helping to keep the great majority of the population obediently in their hamster wheel hatching children, paying interest and generally doing and consuming what they are told without ever really questioning the status quo or trying to fashion a reality of their own.

Some people see the burnout coming and take steps to avoid it, but what started out as a definite change of tack sadly all too often ends up as no more than a transition from one marketing category to another. "Feeling disillusioned sir? I have just the product for you!"

No, thank you.

So that's the tune, but who is it paying the piper? The truth, I would suggest, is not as obvious as it might seem.

The short answer is that the most beautiful dreams are those we do not have to pay for ourselves. This appears at first to confer a clear advantage on those who, by dint of their ability to appeal to our more primal urges, are able to have their fun funded for them. The complicating factor for anyone contemplating this path, however, is that very often both sides will end up knowingly playing the same game – manoeuvring to get what they want without openly appearing to do so – and as a result both will finish up a long way from realizing the dreams they nurtured at the beginning.

As for the long answer, that leads us into hazardous territory and the risk of uncomfortable questions of the type many would no doubt prefer to avoid altogether. The subject of honesty – our willingness (capacity?) to be scrupulously honest with ourselves and with those nearest to us – is a Pandora's Box some would rather have left firmly shut.

My intention here (whisper it softly) is to open this box – with care – and see what it might contain.

RESPONSIBILITY

Social interactions and sociability among sailors were considered in a previous missive, which concluded that frequently it all comes down to ego. A little give here and there can be the unavoidable price of the steady take, take, take and sometimes a veneer of magnanimity helps to oil the wheels of exploitation, but for many, all life centres on me Me ME – and the life afloat is no exception.

One measure of success trumps all others for this mindset and that is wealth, expressed as it may be through symbols such as my partner, my car, my house and my yacht. And the order is by no means coincidental: it takes a particular kind of person to turn the "natural" – pecuniary – order on its head and make a virtue of his or her necessity. It has to be said though that a certain sleight of hand can creep in here:

experts at this game know their audience expects tall tales, so they tell them even taller to make the desired impression! Or so it would seem.

Lies, especially falsehoods concealed behind a painstakingly woven mask of honesty, seem to be just a fact life. Idealistically one might expect advancing years – with the increased financial resources, accumulated experience and evolved view of life's priorities (not to mention a greater willingness to admit our own failings) that tends to accompany them – to change things somewhat. Unfortunately, for this theory at least, intractability increases in step with age and wisdom – that and the certainty that the younger generation has no respect for us and little interest in our knowledge.

Time and again the ego takes centre stage. Impatience rules – who has the time to be understanding (assuming they even know how) – and money is always tight because someone somewhere always has the perfect temptation lined up to part the materially-inclined from every little extra wealth that comes their way. The result, envy, increasingly becomes the driving force of existence, bringing its presence to bear on every decision until trying to satisfy it becomes an end in itself. And one easy short cut to dealing with envy is to go from coveting what others have to denigrating who and what they are (or are perceived to be). What more effortless way could there be to shift the focus away from one's own shortcomings and the woolly countenance looking back in the mirror. Baaaaah!

IS THERE AN EASY ANSWER?

No, in a word. If there was, we would surely have heard about it by now. So where do the resources come from?

This time there are several answers available – read on and take your pick. The ultimate dream, to live your dreams and be paid for doing so, is a kite that should only be flown indoors: expose it to the harsh light of day and jealousy will soon bring it crashing back to earth.

The classic (would-be) exponents of this technique are the sailor-authors, the recognised state of the art being to produce a book summarising the "achievement" (what the rest of us might call the voyage) at the end of the venture. Examples range from thrilling to downright tedious, from honest to almost totally fabricated, from factual to hugely exaggerated (there was even once a book that told of whales but had nothing to show of them but a drawing). The success of a book depends first and foremost on the style in which it is written. The journey, the towering mental anguish and excruciating physical suffering and the eventual heroic return are a given: the question is whether anyone wants to carry on reading all the way to the end. Books can inspire dreams – but not always. Publishers and Jeff Bezos know the score.

Making money out of sailing is an attractive idea –
and an obvious one to anyone looking for ways to
finance time afloat. Unfortunately the probability, as
an author in the maritime genre, of filling the coffers on a scale sufficient to fund a lifetime in what
can hardly be considered a low-cost arena remains
vanishingly small. Writers face a rapidly changing
market too: publishers, struggling to adapt, have no
qualms about placing any financial failure at the feet
of their authors while doing their level best to pare
costs to the bone, chase down every last synergy and
replace expensive experts with the free services of

volunteers and interns in a desperate race to reach the bottom first and survive (after a fashion). Never has the black spot been handed out so freely!

Financing sailing through a website or blog is never easy, as it relies on generating sufficient clicks to attract advertisers and sponsors, who have plenty of choice about where to invest their funds. Something like the VOLVO OCEAN RACE may be able to generate sufficient capital to make the exercise worthwhile, but marketing shiny metal on wheels is a different game altogether to selling boats and associated gear. A sailing race around the world is simply a good way to access all the different markets: the boats are eye-catching but essentially incidental (unless, of course, you happen to be one of the sailors/boatbuilders/sailmakers involved, in which case – well played!).

The right proposition turns the press organs of the world into willing heralds of the brand message. Full-colour high-res images, the "human story": the news flows in almost hourly. And now we have animations too to bring even more of the experience to the sofa. Recast as media partners, elements of the press strain eagerly at the leash for the next carefully prepared titbit, snapping it up and racing to share it with the world: with professional event PR management reducing its role essentially to that of messenger, the press gets cheap content, the event gets the exposure it wants and everyone (who counts) is a winner.

If the pot is big enough, selected press princes/princesses can look forward to free flights, hotel stays and privileged access to help them with their reports – a game that plays out around the world at every host port for events like the ARC without most readers ever being any the wiser. The bill is ultimately footed by the unsuspecting sailors/car buyers who are willing to fork out in pursuit of their dreams (exit through the gift shop).

Sailor-bloggers

operating under the aegis of a publisher – complete with honorarium and assured re-employment – are a hybrid invented by the publishing houses, presumably as a rear-guard action to try and stop themselves being completely overwhelmed by global bloggomania (although bloggers, by their very nature as electronic communicators, must rank as the natural enemy of the paper-based faction).

There is a clear pattern worldwide of bloggers in the privileged position to receive a pecuniary reward from print magazines also being particularly keen on mining the banner ad seam. I suppose it appears the obvious next step: first draw them in and then it's a case of "I'll click yours if you click mine" (at least that must be the plan). The result, as we know to our cost, are click-trap websites where capturing the mouse is everything: once is quite enough!

Compared with the ordinary sailor, who has to shoulder his/her dreams alone with no prospect of a financial return until the writing is done, these hybrid bloggers have it easy. Their financial worries have been smartly offloaded before they so much as hoist a sail and all they have to do in return is report on progress to an interested readership – and not forget to throw in a few timely thank-yous to sponsors and supporters as courtesy, convention and naked self-interest dictate (see here for more thoughts on the matter of sponsorship in sailing).

Which is all perfectly understandable, I suppose, when publishers have but a few horses in the race and can only hazard a guess as to whether the invest-

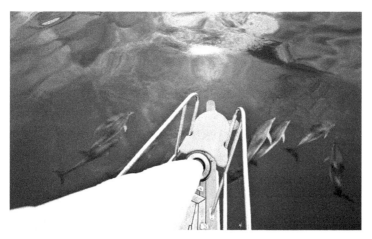

ment in the brand will ultimately pay off. The critical question – which side has the best of the deal – takes a long time to answer because the key facts roll in only slowly. It seems quite possible to me that exploiting the print and online channels in combination will tend to benefit the author rather than the publisher, although the final verdict could be controversial because it will be the latter rather than the former who crunches the numbers and decides.

Experience in Germany has shown that successful long-term alliances between publishers and authors are far from the norm. If I may be so bold, I would suggest that no more than two people have managed to make this arrangement work – and their names will be instantly obvious to the typical German sailor/reader. Whatever their merits, the rest – and plenty have tried – have to face facts and acknowledge that man cannot live by sailing and writing alone.

Digression: Sponsorship

Blogging to sail can create a Bermuda Triangle of conflicting egotistical interests too. Consider if you will the case of a cross-over blogger recently departed on a round-the-world trip (for example) who lets slip a suggestion that money is tight in his reports even though the project's web site appears to be doing a healthy business in collecting financial contributions. One might almost be persuaded to recognise the idea of playing the mariner in need card on a venture already backed by a publishing house plus sponsors and donors – not to mention the beneficiary's own family – as a marketing master stroke, but when everyday issues start regularly to be presented as potential deal-breakers (or, if you prefer, convenient excuses to return to port), one cannot help but by struck by the yawning gulf between the mighty marketing effort and the underwhelming commitment of the "hero". Especially given the clear implication that it is the generosity or otherwise of sponsors and donors that will make the difference between sailing on and sailing straight back home. Are they laughing at us, I wonder?

Moving now into a completely different league in terms of elegance, we turn to the option of setting sail with Daddy's boat (or Daddy's assets in boat form) once Daddy, worn down by years of hard graft, finds that ill health, financial crisis or the dearly be-loved family have driven a barge through his plans and he is no longer able to realise his life's dream himself. Daddy's loss is fortunate son's or daughter's gain – and it never ceases to amaze me how quickly awe, respect and gratitude for the efforts of diligent parents dissipate at sea and how shamelessly the offspring acquire a swagger and self-confidence that can be difficult not to interpret as arrogance.

These sorts of thoughts put me in mind of an eye-opening day I once spent in Las Palmas: I was doing my thing upgrading the back end of a yacht when the owner's son appeared in the cockpit and asked my partner to remove herself from the shade of his bi-mini and find somewhere ashore to wait. The 17 mm wrench in my hand came pretty close to a watery grave, believe me, but I stayed cool and kept things polite – a failing I rue to this day!

Strangely though, putting the experience down in words has brought a fleeting smile to my face...

I have noticed that the self-confidence of these silver spooners grows at a rate inversely proportio-nal to their own achievements in life. And I have also noted a not insignificant number of instances in which parents, having worked hard all their life to build a thriving business, hand over the reins to the next generation and set sail for the sun only to find, a few months down the line, that the golden eggs have stopped, the goose is on its last legs and the only hope is to race home double-quick and try to minimise the damage. Which can be a tall order indeed.

Such are the perils of success accompanied by re-production!

Mixing family and sailing does not have to result in conflict/exploitation of course. Parents and their adult children can and do undertake bluewater trips together as family – family yacht Kire covered many thousands of miles as home to Erik Jörn and has also taken his son Paul and family around the world, for example. These happy exceptions seem to be in short supply though, which is a pity, not least because they offer significant financial advantages – two generations obviously have more earning power – and also extract more value from the boat, which spends far less time straining impatiently at its lines in port.

I have a particular respect for sailors capable of travelling the globe with a smile, a wave and no mention of the state of their finances. Catching up with the latest exploits of Inga and Vassil on Olgalou is always a pleasure, for example, and I am always happy to do whatever I can to help them (see also here). Inga has certainly helped me – and hopefully you – too, as it is from her pen that the cartoons enlivening much of my writing flow.

Big in America (although less so in Germany) are sailor-bloggers who sell their books and reports direct and live off the proceeds (for a list of sailor-bloggers see here). I anticipate imminent and dramatic change in the market for German-language writing – be it in print or online – on sailing matters. In fact the storm clouds are already gathering: if the prices of e-books drop to the levels that have become established for apps (with the beneficiary, similarly, being the actual author), public interest will increase rapidly and authors will find they have a reasonable business on their hands at the same time as the publishers, their print sales figures dropping steadily, struggle more and more even to cover their costs.

We already hear regular stories about the upheaval in the print media industry and I am on tenterhooks to find out what strategies the barons of the old world of print will come up with to keep themselves afloat as our sweet little marine publishing segment moves into a digital age they seem incapable of understanding. Evidence of the prevailing panic is everywhere to be seen, with each new round of consolidation following closely on the heels of the last, but it seems far from certain that all of this feverish activity will make any difference. I find it hard to envisage print sales recovering in any great measure: the print media could well become an irrelevance in our field (but stand down the chainsaws for now – the tree does still bear fruit occasionally).

Many of the authors can be found here

The state of the art

Most of us plan and fund our sailing adventures ourselves. How long it takes to advance from concept to implementation depends on all kinds of factors like how far we intend to go, how quickly and comfortably we intend to travel and what else we think we need to make the experience a success.

There seems little point in discussing the actual costs of boats because everyone has their own idea of "boat". The literature and the supply of would-be advisors is immense and there have even been studies conducted to determine, retrospectively, the annual cost of living a particular dream. And as far as I can see all of these efforts have one thing in common: they become totally irrelevant as soon as the first halyard moves.

But anyway, how much should it cost to realise the dream? Few things are as sure to spark heated debate among established and prospective bluewater sailors as the quest to put a number on this issue. The answers, not surprisingly, vary as widely as the expectations, aspirations and lifestyles of those who put to sea, so for now I will focus on just three key factors:
 – the boat
 – life
 – income, assets and reserves.

I suspect very few people would be happy to open the books and reveal their true costs simply because the whole issue immediately conjures the green-eyed monster of envy. And in any case the breakdowns of the actual costs of circumnavigators published in table form at the end of the adventure can never give more than a very rough indication because, as we all know, one man's boat is another man's tender, one woman's luxury is another woman's squalor and there's just no accounting for luck. Sensible people can safely be left to work out their own budget.

Vast wealth is no guarantee of success. Much more important, I feel, is the ability to recognise what really matters in life – and what does not. Which thought brings me directly to Doris Zulauf and Andreas Bitterli (Andori): a more compelling and authentic voice on our sport than this couple, who took their Taranga all the way around the world (with all the ups, downs and challenges one would expect this to entail) with no more than a modest budget, you could not hope to find. Or take Barbara and Hans Rauert (Resolute): they crossed their outbound track last year to complete the full circle and remain as upbeat and grounded as ever, rising to the mental challenge of ticking that big box by ... recharging, restocking, and carrying on sailing.

Murphy's Law has no respect for national frontiers and it is impossible to predict if/when something expensive is going to happen: stuff breaks, people fall ill, sometimes people just need to jump on a plane home and check in with friends and family before the next leg of the voyage.

IN CONCLUSION

I've blogged it before and I may well blog it again: the world – and with it our world of long-distance sailing – has changed. People have changed as well, at least there seems to be rather more egocentricity around than there used to be. Security has become more of a concern too, with piracy much more common and envy and theft almost ubiquitous.

Changes in personal circumstances, illness and family emergencies certainly also do their bit to rewrite the best laid bluewater plans, but probably the greatest challenge for bluewater sailors at the moment is loss of income due to flat-lining interest rates. Sailors tend in my observation to be conservative with their money, not least I suppose because it is difficult to monitor and manage fast-moving speculative investments from the middle of the ocean. It is surely no accident that recent years have seen so many bluewater sailors put their plans on hold, sell their boat halfway around or just ship it home as deck cargo. Anyone requiring further evidence need look no further than the collapse in prices for big yachts.

Not so long ago, people could save up ahead of the Big Trip and then fund themselves largely out of interest income. Those days are over now, for the time being at least, and I am sure this goes a long way to explaining why so many sailors, remembering that they will still have a life to finance when they get back on dry land, are rethinking their plans and goals.

THE GENIE IN THE BOTTLE

My advice, for what it's worth, is never to proclaim (admit) in advance that you intend to sail all the way around: showing your cards precipitately ratchets up the pressure of personal and outside expectation unnecessarily. Once at sea, you want to be able to experience and enjoy every day as it comes without feeling the weight of expectation – or envy – from those you have left behind and without finding yourself pushing on simply to avoid disappointing your well-wishers, proving the naysayers right or breaking what has come to be seen as a promise.

Once the genie of conflicting social pressures slips out of the bottle it permeates everything in the ship's paradise, even relations between Adam and Eve. A life without dreams would be barely a life at all, but sharing your dreams too widely can leave you in debt to them. Sailors, like other dreamers, are not immune to the temptation of publicising great plans as a means of therapy for a needy ego, but a declared circumnavigation that terminates short of the full distance will be perceived as a defeat even if the journey itself was wonderful.

We struggle sometimes to acknowledge what others have achieved without simultaneously pointing out where they have come up short. Whatever our preconceptions and however events play out, there remains a voice at the back of our head that always wants to find a way to be able to say: "See, I told you so!"

Well sometimes anyway!

Peter Foerthmann

CIRCUMNAVIGATION # 4

HOME AGAIN
... AND THEN WHAT?

The last few miles pass in a flash and then it's a head-long plunge into a joyous, welcoming throng of loved-ones, friends and family. Even ancient distant relations never normally to be seen anywhere near the sea make an exception and put in an appearance. There follow scattered moments of bliss, a few tears, much waving, popping of corks and draining of bottles and a fair smattering of "We must catch up properly soon".

Family life resumes, in other words, at first probably in a kinder, gentler form with unprecedented levels of harmony and none of the usual jockeying for position: you have been gone long enough to be genuinely missed (if not forgotten). But fitting long-time absentees back into the established social structure is a process with winners and losers ...

Hopes and expectations unfold against an under-current of reproach, a feeling that those who flew the coop voluntarily should not necessarily assume immediate and painless readmission. Mutual respect and understanding are essential if the reintegration

process is to be completed without tempers flaring and those who find themselves displaced to accommodate sailors, once gone and now returned, moved to give a full and frank exposition of their feelings.

Going to sea can open a rift in the social fabric, reanimating old grievances and inspiring new ones (and some of the aggrieved will inevitably seize on the moment of return as the perfect moment to settle old scores). I am reminded once again that while our partner may be our own achievement, we have the rest of our family thrust upon us. The media may like to try and tell us otherwise (if it sells), but while most people will have no great difficulty enticing family to turn up for a party, far fewer could honestly rank their relatives among their friends.

Anyway, sooner or later the welcome party draws to a close and everyone heads home to their comfortable bed. And it is a bed – a real one with a head, a foot and two sides – and it will be comfortable; in fact thanks to our innate gift for always seeing the grass on the other side through green-tinted spectacles, even the meanest of land-based accommodation will seem positively palatial compared to the still-ever-so-slightly-damp confines of the boat.

The last night on board leads directly into the enthusiastic clear-out and the ritual trial of transporting too much stuff in too few trolleys and then trying to load it into the car while still leaving space for the people. And then – drum roll please – it happens: the zero hour, tabula rasa, the first day of the rest of your life with dry land beneath your feet.

How it plays out in practice seems to depend largely on the bigger picture: some people step ashore with dreams realised and a fair idea of where to go next; others with at least mixed feelings about the past and nothing but uncharted territory ahead. The morning after the night before can be a shock without adequate mental preparation.

Those returnees who still have their own four walls have a great advantage here: dump the yachting paraphernalia somewhere out of sight, open the windows, brush off the dust, fire up the heating if necessary and boom: you are ready to go. Those who really do have to start again from scratch have it much harder: even once you have found a place to live it takes effort to turn it into home and a long time before it inspires any sense of belonging. And all the while the thought remains: down there at the waterside, tugging hopefully at its moorings, bobs the passport to an alternative future ready and waiting for another adventure.

So, what next? My intention in writing this is to discuss and examine – in a hopefully humorous way and with absolutely no desire to imply any kind of value judgement – which elements of life's rich tapestry often come to assume an unanticipated importance for the sailor returning and which have to be put out

of mind for want of time to prepare properly when keeping the boat going is so much more pressing.

While every case is different and care must be taken to ensure comparisons are valid, generally speaking it makes a big difference whether the round-the-world trip takes place mid- or post-career and, of course, how much time it consumes.

STIMULUS AND RESPONSE

The causes, implications and consequences of the decision to embark on The Big One could hardly be more varied, especially as they involve and impact on whole families. Parents who decide at a relatively young age and for purely egotistical – if entirely understandable – reasons to give up a professional career that today's uncertain labour market may well prevent them from ever resuming run a considerable risk. The risk assessments on which we base the decisions that shape our life remain sovereign territory, but the consequences of a misjudgement in this department are much more serious than they used to be. It appears more and more people are stepping ashore to find that in working life at least, resuming where they left off is simply not an option. A career break can be a significant impediment with competition for jobs so fierce, ever higher expectations with regard to personal development and qualifications and the need to demonstrate an extensive and unbroken record of professional achievement. Specialists possessed of the sort of expertise that always holds its value have a clear edge here, as they will usually be able to slot straight back into place, possibly even with the same employer. Least vulnerable of all in this context are those who have built their working life around independence, as they really can return to business as usual – provided they maintain their contacts properly while away.

Sailing around the world in the middle of working life generally involves a prolonged career break: there's just too far to go and too much to see to manage it within a sabbatical.

Sharing the experience with children can give them a wonderful head-start in life, however. Kids usually come back thoroughly enriched by the whole adventure: more knowledgeable about the world than their peers, more skilled in communication, undaunted by change and novelty, more self-assured and decidedly more independent.

SOCIAL TIES

Long-distance sailors occupy a special position in the social web of family and friends by virtue of their itinerant lifestyle and their propensity – immune to all forms of logical or emotional persuasion – to drop off the scene for months and years on end. The decision to go, to cast off, set sail and return who knows when brings a moment of truth in family relationships, revealing how much mutual respect really exists between family members and how willing individuals are to compromise on their own desires and expectations.

The repercussions can be even stronger for parents of adult children, born, raised, schooled and graduated, who decide the hour has finally come to move on with their own life and leave their offspring to explore an independent future. The kids, accustomed to the notion that they have the old folks well trained, don't always like the idea. Families of course can be competitive places and I am aware of several cases in which the start of the great voyage and the associated unavoidable loosening of ties proved a welcome release for all sides (in some instances with quite unforeseeable results).

We are accustomed to hearing family ties described in solemn, sacred tones but does this really reflect reality on the ground? It seems in many families that these fine words represent no more than a reflex, a habit, a borrowed collection of platitudes concealing a reality in which true solidarity remains a scarce commodity and successfully installing a respectable next generation without falling victim to any of the countless family battles to be fought along the way remains a mighty challenge. Nothing brings out the true state of family cohesion like the distribution of assets. Who sits where for dinner on the big occasions may be contentious, but it pales beside questions like who gets the house, who gets the family silver and who – whisper it gently – gets the boat. Word has reached me of families in which the parents have taken a thorough emotional beating for having the audacity to fritter away the proceeds of their life's work on their own remaining years (afloat, naturally) without first obtaining the permission of their heirs.

The corollary of this, of course, is that there can hardly be a better way for parents to underline to the offspring that even Mum and Dad still deserve – and intend to have – a life of their own and that there comes a time when everyone needs to stand on their own two feet. The day the parents announce they're going to sea brings a moment of truth for any family.

TIES TO HOME

All the communications wizardry in the world cannot prevent ties to home growing steadily weaker
with each passing day away. Often contact is eventually lost with all but close family – and even there
life goes on and the physical remoteness of sailors
effectively living in a different world leaves an unmistakeable imprint. The peculiar tension between
different generations habituated to living cheek by
jowl ensures a steady supply of meticulously craf-
ted reproaches. And with reproach comes guilt, that
constant companion on life's journey. Physical distance makes these barbs incomparably more effec-
tive such that sometimes brushing them aside ceases to be an option and a line in the sand has to be
drawn. Nobody can outrun a constant hail of repro-
achful comments forever: you either take a stand or
accept that eventually these verbal smart bombs will
begin to take their toll. Sound defence is always the
best policy!

A permanent guilty conscience does nobody any
good, least of all the type of person who has probably
always done their best only to discover, in later life,
that their best is not good enough to spare them the
reproach of dissatisfied descendants. There exists a
mindset according to which the blame can always be
made to lie with the other person: it's just a case of

working out why, making the accusation stick and then hoping he or she doesn't put up a fight... People whose horizons have drawn in to nothing more than Me and Mine can be truly, truly awful.

SEPARATION AS EPIPHANY?

Periods of separation focus attention on the essential. Everything else just fades away into the background. More than a few sailors have discovered on their return that they no longer have much to say to former friends, which perhaps begs the question: was it ever really any different? A sailing trip as the cue for an epiphany? Perfectly conceivable.

I have made the acquaintance of sailors whose address book shrank and shrank until in the end they remained in contact only with immediate family – and then only with the status of near-outlaws.

FRIENDS

A prolonged absence changes relationships even with long-standing friends. I suspect the people left behind with no grand plans of their own when a friend sets off on a great adventure often cannot help but develop a certain measure of envy. The fact that the returning mariner almost always comes home profoundly moved by the whole experience and suffused with an irrepressible urge to talk about it (in exhaustive detail) hardly smooths the waters either.

It is noticeable that sailors returning from a serious long-distance venture often go on to cultivate contacts with other well-travelled sailors, with whom they can discuss and reflect on shared experiences properly as equals, as it were, and meet with much greater understanding than can be expected with people who have never tested the bounds of their comfort zone to a comparable extent.

These friendships among apparently like-minded bluewater veterans can turn awkward though: there always seem to be a few seafaring contemporaries who consider it rather good fun to invite themselves for a visit with old "friends" and then take up residence in the guest room for as long as possible. Such problems do not arise in the same way on the water: visitors have their own home riding at anchor not so far away, so everything can be much more casual. Visits on land intrude much more fully into your own living space – your house, bathrooms and bedrooms – and expose you to much more of your guests (complete with all accompanying noises and smells). How much honesty can a person bear in these circumstances? My wife has devised her own simple rule: after three hours fish and visits begin to impinge on the nose, personal freedom begins to feel constrained and attentive curiosity begins to wane. Sensitive and considerate visitors, of course, are a different matter. Mutual respect can quickly be established if people have the confidence to speak their mind. Politeness is one thing, but nobody has any fun if everyone feels they are walking on eggshells.

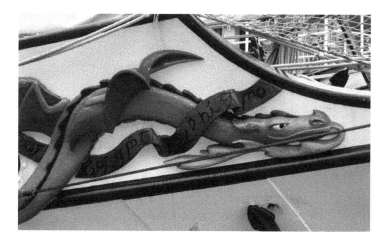

IN SUMMARY

Partners who have survived sailing around the world together are ideally prepared to share whatever challenges the rest of life has in store for them: there is precious little on land capable of shaking foundations that have withstood the trials of a life at sea.

Circumnavigating amicably with a partner as a team of two is an intense experience that creates a tight bond between the couple involved while simultaneously distancing them from those left ashore. Time at sea infuses a sense of perspective not always appreciated or understood by uninitiated friends and relatives, who may be found to seek solace in jealousy.

Still, we cannot hope to please everyone all the time so perhaps a little more realism is in order: manage to be happy in your own skin and a large part of the battle is already won...

suggests
Peter Foerthmann

CIRCUMNAVIGATION # 5

EPILOGUE – CORONAVIRUS
THE TURNING POINT?

Having been in the game for several decades, I can report with some authority that while the dream of circumnavigating may be as captivating as ever for would-be bluewater adventurers straining at the leash of everyday life, the classic notion of absolute, unlimited freedom can no longer be reconciled with the reality. Gone with the wind are the days when we could put to sea free as a bird, more or less – or not at all – prepared and revel in that space to breathe and roam unfettered that so many find so sorely lacking on land. The plan of one day stepping aboard, hoisting the sails and leaving familiar land, responsibilities and worries far behind was like a valve that one could open in time of need – assuming one had the courage and, of course, a boat tough enough to cope with the world of adventure that awaited. Just set off and do it, every day a new surprise, every day a new discovery ... And today?

credit Vlado Porvaznik

The world has become smaller and rather safer for sailors far from home thanks to the ready availability of good weather information that enables us to sail in weather windows and dodge the worst meteorological excesses, to radar and AIS that help us track and keep clear of other water users – from rafts to supertankers – whatever the visibility and to services like Iridium and the ubiquity of the internet that make it possible for us to keep in touch, research countries, people and relevant authorities on the move and complete arrival and departure forms electronically in advance (this may not make all that much difference to the actual time spent on sweltering dusty quaysides dealing with official formalities, but the wait for essential stamps or passes in picturesque locations far from home tends not to drag as it ordinarily would because it fits naturally into the overall experience). Should the urge arise, we can even check out the walking distance to the nearest bakeries and study their user reviews and ratings.

We have grown accustomed to life on social networks, learned the rules and how to play the game and need never be truly alone no matter how far we range. One thing the online world cannot do for us, however, is keep the boat going: for all that electronic gadgets are as much a part of cruising today as sheets and halyards, ultimately we are still absolutely reliant on our own sailing ability and resourcefulness.

It is part and parcel of our bold voyaging that we keep a thriving community of engineers and replacement part logistics companies in business: rare indeed is the boat on which everything works properly all the time! Sometimes our interactions with this community can give the impression of helping to build understanding among the peoples of the earth, but the truth, I suspect, is that the itinerant sailor always remains an outsider. The mortar that really binds us together is always money – the money the one has and the other would like to obtain, be it with goods and services or, as the case may be, by relieving us of the dinghy in the small hours of the night.

Experience has taught us to give unsafe coasts a wide berth, to be aware of and to respect social tensions and to trust our gut feeling if it tells us to disappear in a hurry. The bush telegraph seems to work particularly well in popular anchorages, quickly spreading word of whatever it is everyone needs to know. Like it or not, the latest news seems to find its way aboard almost as soon as the hook is set (aided and abetted by our enthusiasm for gossip and social contact from beyond our own microhabitat).

Sailors who hear the call of blue water but find their faith in their ability to cope alone dwindling rapidly as the shoreline recedes need not despair thanks to the rise of flotilla events – "guided sailing" – that provide a comprehensive, all-inclusive service in exchange for a healthy slice of the yacht's budget. These events descend on far-flung harbours like a swarm of locusts, completely dominating the scene until the day comes to head for the next stop on the list and peace returns for the rest of the year.

Sailors who struggle with time rather than self-reliance also have an easy solution at hand in the form of the ready-to-sail charter fleets that have sprung up all over the place: fly in, jump aboard, cast off, take some photos in this or that idyllic bay, breathe deep the fragrant air, ruffle the sand on an exotic beach or two, devour some photogenic seafood and generally unload a few months' worth of stress before leaping back onto the hamster wheel refreshed, reanimated and eager for the next time. It's all about fitting as much as possible into the limited hours available, ergonomically, economically and ... egonomically. The fleets are large, the available destinations plentiful, the airports never too far from the dock, all things curated to create the right look, it doesn't take long to search, click and book.

Or might a cruise ship be the better alternative? All the balloons and fanfare, plenty of opportunity for fine frocks and a new wonder to gaze upon every morning when the curtains silently part – guaranteed! Unsure of your sea legs? Fear not: stabilisers are installed to keep everything level in a swell and make sure the false teeth don't slide off the counter in the night. Unless the power goes off, of course, in which case the pod drives shut down leaving the whole giant sardine tin liable to drift beam on to the waves until the shaking parts the furniture from the floor. There's worse too: who can ever forget those images of the Costa Concordia and the nightmare tale of what can happen when an ill-judged cornering manoeuvre pits sheet metal against the submerged sharp end of a sizeable island?

It could have carried on like this, business as usual forever. But then 2020 arrived and business as usual became most unusual. We have grit in the gears; the broadcast has been interrupted. Hence this epilogue.

The fleet-wise movements of recreational sailors have grown and grown in recent times, placing increasing pressure on popular destinations and their waters. While the Earth rotates to the East, sailing traffic moves in the opposite direction to minimise the time spent with inconvenient headwinds. The avalanche of boats cresting the Atlantic thins out somewhat West of Panama, with very few squeezing around the corner at Cape Town (word is around 140 international boats entered the Atlantic via the Cape of Good in July 2020). Eight to ten times as many boats transit the Panama Canal every year as make it back past South Africa, so there must have been some profound revision of plans going on somewhere along the way even before the pandemic.

A painstaking breakdown of global yacht movements in 2015 based on data presumably sourced from the customs authorities revealed all kinds of surprises. Who would have guessed that the delights of Hawaii consistently draw in only a few dozen visiting yachts a year, for example? Too far to go for a hula skirt?

credit Wolfgang Wappl

The question of where all the boats go after Panama remains one of the mysteries of our time. The options are numerous and no word has yet reached Hamburg of a Bermuda triangle in the Pacific. A prompt airlift home via transport helicopter can safely be ruled out too, although it is far from unprecedented these days for the crew to fly back and entrust their boat to a shipping company for later delivery home. Netherlands-based Sevenstar alone has a 120-strong fleet of specialist yacht transport ships shifting armadas of boats between primary hubs around the world (the African continent excluded). The convenience of shipping the ship has made this a popular option where budgets allow, especially as paid crew can use the downtime to catch up on servicing, painting and polishing work.

The system creates a win-win-win scenario for owners who are able to visit the most beautiful spots on the planet one after another, condense the great global tour into a series of monthly excursions and take on the mantle of circumnavigator without, strictly speaking, having sailed around the world. Even some of the renowned sailing greats have been known to piggyback on a freighter to keep up with a challenging schedule – not that they're likely to brag about it.

In a world in which benefits are constantly at the mercy of costs, Sevenstar's dependable timetable has become an affordable alternative for many. The ships themselves make quite a spectacle too as they steam into Martinique, Ft. Lauderdale or wherever, partially submerge, load/unload their floating cargo, emerge once more from the waters and steam off back over the horizon again. Crazy times! But all good economic sense too, depending on one's perspective.

credit Gerard Dykstra

Bottlenecks like the Northwest Passage homewards and the alternatives of Cape Horn or the Strait of Magellan are thoroughly hardcore options restricted to dedicated seadogs and contemporaries looking to include a special highlight in the programme for paying guests or add a unique selling point to their own personal legend. A well-insulated yacht rated for use in the ice and equipped with a dual-heater system is essential at these latitudes. Another short cut, relative to the conventional routes at least, is the Suez Canal. Heating is certainly irrelevant here, but a strong hull – ideally armour-plated – backed up by an even stronger nerve (and a most diligent guardian angel) will be essential given the risk of hostile encounters.

credit Douwe Fokkema

Full marinas at the main points of landfall and the sheer number of boats in this part of the world appearing on the brokers' for sale lists tend to suggest the majority of crews setting out on the long trek westwards throw in the towel along the way. This, I must stress, is more or less how it was before Covid 19!

Now the world is holding its breath – especially in confined spaces and whenever anyone coughs. Breathing has become one of those things we actively think about in life, a life in which almost everything we took for granted has been upended and we can no longer avoid a humble acknowledgement of our ultimate insignificance.

The situation at the time of writing (July 2020) is that coronavirus has pretty much halted the blue-water activity – dreams and reality alike – described above. Everything has changed. It is difficult (!) to predict what the future holds for the international cruising community, but having done my best to see through the fog of the events of recent months and studied the reports of a large number of sailors, I think it is possible to pick out some potentially informative trends and developments.

We couldn't quite believe the tragedy unfolding in far-away Wuhan would reach our own towns and streets and the scale of the lockdown tsunami it triggered when it did is hard to comprehend even now. Which side of the wheel of fortune the many voyaging sailors around the world found themselves nailed to when coronavirus arrived came down to timing alone. Virtually all sailing activity worldwide ground to a halt, with the only exceptions being those few sailors already far from land who simply carried on ticking off the miles – with impeccable social distancing of course – until eventually reaching land to find (bureaucracy willing) that their weeks of self-isolation at sea would spare them the need to quarantine.

Many sailors saw the pot of gold at the end of their rainbow, the time in paradise on the other side of the world that motivates so many, brutally snatched away from them. The situation in French Polynesia soured dramatically as routine things like a trip to the doctor suddenly became impossible, food prices shot up and fresh goods became so scarce they could only be purchased once a week. Reports from sailors in the region reveal a roller-coaster of emotions ranging from disbelief at the unexpected things that have suddenly become essential (and scarce) to a desire to buy a plot of land and stay forever in the knowledge that unanticipated difficulties await in every direction and all options in terms of future destinations are out of the question due to quarantine measures. With otherwise safe anchorages now hugely overcrowded, hair-raising anchor watches a nightly routine rather than a rare exception and relations with the local population very strained due to competition for food in the supermarket, it isn't difficult to imagine how sailors stranded thousands of miles from the relative security of home in what was supposed to be paradise might be feeling. Dreams years and decades in the crafting have been reduced to ash.

credit Tino Schumann

I know of sailors who terminated their travels through paradise on the spot, cleared the boat, handed it over to a broker to sell and headed straight home as soon as the first flights returned to the air.

Some sailors cruising in New Zealand when the music stopped have gone incognito, even taking their online presence down, to avoid attracting attention from the authorities. The sailing community has quietly come together in response to shared concerns and the universal question of what next.

Reports from Honolulu speak of a relatively mild lockdown, although even here the changes made in an otherwise pulsating tourist haven would have been unimaginable until recently. Liveaboards on the island are apparently planning to carry on sailing.

One German liveaboard traversed the remote Malay Archipelago, constantly on guard to avoid unwelcome inspections, before recently reaching a satisfactory harbour and parking his boat to fly home.

The crew of a US-flagged yacht who risked the short cut through the Red Sea to the Med on the way back from India looked on in horror as an unmanned drone, in the form of an open fishing boat with conspicuously powerful engines, shadowed their Beneteau at a distance of just a few metres before apparently deciding they weren't worth the trouble of sinking. Their circumnavigation, which began in Boston in December 2018, ended back home 18 months later without another landfall.

Countless yachts inbound from St. Helena chose to head directly to Europe, which makes for a very, very long sail.

There were dramatic scenes in the Caribbean as hundreds of sailors fleeing the more northerly islands in search of a safer anchorage and somewhere to weigh their options before hurricane season found themselves struggling to squeeze into already crowded bays in the less vulnerable southerly destinations.

Thanks to the selfless efforts of the Salty Dawg Sailing Association, 252 boats were able to be moved to safer waters to the North. Some sailors who were not able to move their boat South faced surcharges from their insurer. I'm not sure I should mention it, but one German crew even sought help from the German Federal Foreign Office. They were apparently to ashamed to give their real names ...

One particularly eye-catching update came from the American skipper of a Swan 48, a long-standing fixture of the scene, who shared a sober account of his unpleasant experiences with local authorities in a place in which he had been a familiar and appreciated presence for decades. This is a man who contributed enormously to the rebuilding of St. Maarten after the devastation of Hurricane Irma and surely had every right to expect a sympathetic hearing. What he received instead was a curt visit on his boat from the local customs telling him to leave immediately and an escort out of territorial waters to ensure that he did just that. The story even made waves in the USA.

The list of extraordinary experiences to have come bluewater sailors' way so far this year is almost endless: everyone out there afloat has their own unique story to tell. One factor common to all the accounts I have seen is the sailors' ability to respond flexibly and adapt to the new situation. Sailors of course are used to finding ways to master novel challenges with just the resources to hand and are thus probably better suited to coping in our changing world than people unaccustomed to making decisions with consequences on their own. It seems to me that despite the North Atlantic conjuring up several bouts of lively weather to complicate matters this year, sailors making their way back to European shores have done a good job in the circumstances.

The pandemic has certainly deflated the dream of freedom at sea for the time being but it will never puncture the passion for sailing shared by all of us with salt water in our veins. Distance – and even isolation – are inherent in our sport, as is the ability to keep an eye on the bigger picture. We understand too that all over the world it is people who create the greatest hazards and we love the opportunity that sailing brings to leave all of that behind and, for a while at least, to live an independent life according to our own rules. It is second nature for us to synchronise our travel plans with meteorological developments, to monitor geopolitical developments carefully to avoid threats to our vessel and crew and to accept that there are certain parts of the world we have no business visiting.

We will doubtless adapt our plans and objectives to the new situation. Perhaps we will explore our local areas more thoroughly and discover wonderful, previously overlooked corners on our own side of the ocean. Perhaps too we will rein in our yearning for far-flung destinations somewhat given that reaching them very often means flying and flying, as travellers around the world are starting to realise, means breathing in air that is not ours alone.

Embracing personal responsibility comes naturally to sailors: people unwilling or unable to take this step are unlikely ever to leave the shore. It's that old story of the wheat and the chaff again ...

26.07.2020
Peter Foerthmann

Lightning Source UK Ltd.
Milton Keynes UK
UKHW021451051120
372836UK00001B/49